DINGO VS. KANGAROO

BY KIERAN DOWNS

BELLWETHER MEDIA • MINNEAPOLIS, MN

TM

Torque brims with excitement
perfect for thrill-seekers of all kinds.
Discover daring survival skills, explore
uncharted worlds, and marvel at mighty
engines and extreme sports. In *Torque* books,
anything can happen. Are you ready?

This edition first published in 2022 by Bellwether Media, Inc.

No part of this publication may be reproduced in whole or in part without written
permission of the publisher. For information regarding permission, write to
Bellwether Media, Inc., Attention: Permissions Department,
6012 Blue Circle Drive, Minnetonka, MN 55343.

Library of Congress Cataloging-in-Publication Data

Names: Downs, Kieran, author.
Title: Dingo vs. kangaroo / by Kieran Downs.
Description: Minneapolis, MN : Bellwether Media, 2022. | Series: Torque:
  Animal battles | Includes bibliographical references and index. |
  Audience: Ages 7-12 | Audience: Grades 4-6 | Summary: "Amazing
  photography accompanies engaging information about the fighting
  abilities of dingoes and kangaroos. The combination of high-interest
  subject matter and light text is intended for students in grades 3
  through 7"– Provided by publisher.
Identifiers: LCCN 2021001453 (print) | LCCN 2021001454 (ebook) | ISBN
  9781644875322 (library binding) | ISBN 9781648344947 (paperback) | ISBN
  9781648344404 (ebook)
Subjects: LCSH: Dingo–Juvenile literature. | Kangaroos–Juvenile literature.
Classification: LCC QL737.C22 D695 2022 (print) | LCC QL737.C22 (ebook) |
  DDC 599.77/2–dc23
LC record available at https://lccn.loc.gov/2021001453
LC ebook record available at https://lccn.loc.gov/2021001454

Editor: Rebecca Sabelko   Designer: Josh Brink

Printed in the United States of America, North Mankato, MN.

TABLE OF CONTENTS

THE COMPETITORS

Australia is home to some of the toughest animals in the world. Dingoes hunt in packs across the land. These **predators** have strength in numbers.

But predators are not the only animals with natural weapons. Kangaroos fight with powerful kicks. Who would win this Australian battle?

DINGO PROFILE

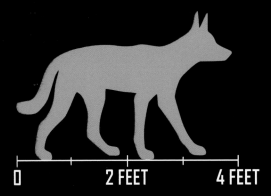

0   2 FEET   4 FEET

LENGTH
UP TO 3.9 FEET
(1.2 METERS)

WEIGHT
UP TO 44 POUNDS
(20 KILOGRAMS)

HABITAT

PLAINS

DESERTS

MOUNTAINS

FORESTS

DINGO RANGE

■ RANGE

Dingoes are wild dogs found in Australia and Southeast Asia. They live in many **habitats** such as forests, **plains**, mountains, and deserts.

These dogs have bushy tails and short, red-brown fur. Dingoes live in packs that usually have around 10 members. They are highly **territorial** and will fight off anyone who is not welcome.

BIG DOGS

Dingoes are the largest land predators in Australia!

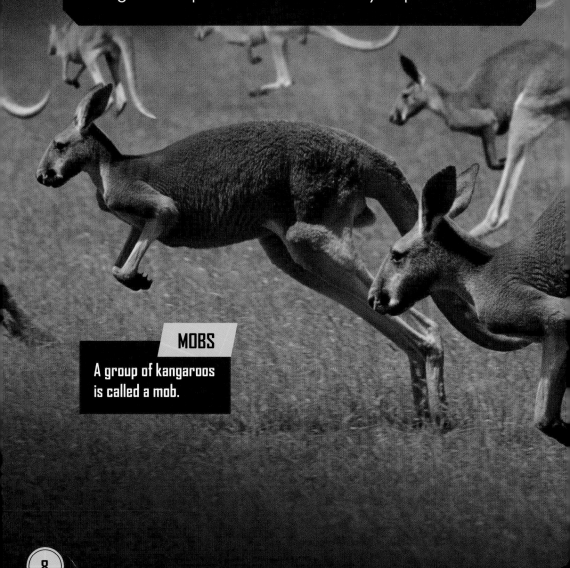

Kangaroos are **marsupials**. They keep their young in pouches on their stomachs. There are three main kangaroo **species** in Australia. They live in deserts and grasslands.

Kangaroos usually stand and move on their hind legs. They bounce on both legs at the same time. Their long, strong tails help them balance as they hop.

MOBS

A group of kangaroos is called a mob.

RED KANGAROO PROFILE

WEIGHT
UP TO 200 POUNDS
(91 KILOGRAMS)

HEIGHT
UP TO 5.25 FEET
(1.6 METERS)

6 FEET
5 FEET
4 FEET
3 FEET
2 FEET
1 FOOT

HABITAT

DESERT

GRASSLAND

RED KANGAROO RANGE

█ RANGE

SECRET WEAPONS

Dingoes are skilled hunters with many
weapons. Their mouths are filled with sharp
teeth. Large **canine teeth** cut into **prey**.
Wide jaws allow them to take big bites!

Kangaroos have sharp, curved claws on their hands and feet. Their claws are used to grab food and groom fur. They are also dangerous weapons. They can cause deep cuts.

DINGO TOP SPEED

37 MILES (60 KILOMETERS) PER HOUR

DINGO

28 MILES (45 KILOMETERS) PER HOUR

HUMAN

Dingoes chase down their prey. They can reach speeds of up to 37 miles (60 kilometers) per hour!

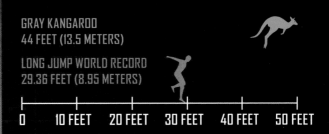

GRAY KANGAROO LEAPING DISTANCE

GRAY KANGAROO
44 FEET (13.5 METERS)

LONG JUMP WORLD RECORD
29.36 FEET (8.95 METERS)

| 0 | 10 FEET | 20 FEET | 30 FEET | 40 FEET | 50 FEET |

HIGH JUMP

Red kangaroos can jump up to
10 feet (3 meters) in the air!

Kangaroos have powerful hind legs.
Their legs let them jump long distances.
They can leap more than 44 feet
(13.5 meters) in a single jump!

SECRET WEAPONS

SHARP TEETH

SPEED

JUMPING

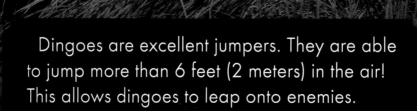

Dingoes are excellent jumpers. They are able to jump more than 6 feet (2 meters) in the air! This allows dingoes to leap onto enemies.

SECRET WEAPONS

SHARP CLAWS

STRONG LEGS

LARGE EARS

Kangaroos' large ears help them hear well. Each ear can follow a sound on its own. This lets kangaroos hear enemies that approach from all directions.

ATTACK MOVES

Dingoes often hunt small animals. They catch prey in their teeth. Then they quickly shake their heads to finish off their prey.

Kangaroos kick with both powerful hind legs at the same time. Each blow has up to 759 pounds (344 kilograms) of **force**! They lean on their tails to help them kick hard.

A dingo's skull is the widest part of its body. This lets it know that if its head fits through an opening, the rest of its body will too!

Dingoes hunt large prey in packs. The pack circles the prey. Then it attacks! When the prey falls, the pack tears it apart.

Kangaroos attack with their arms. They will slap and grab their enemies. This gives kangaroos time to deliver a kick.

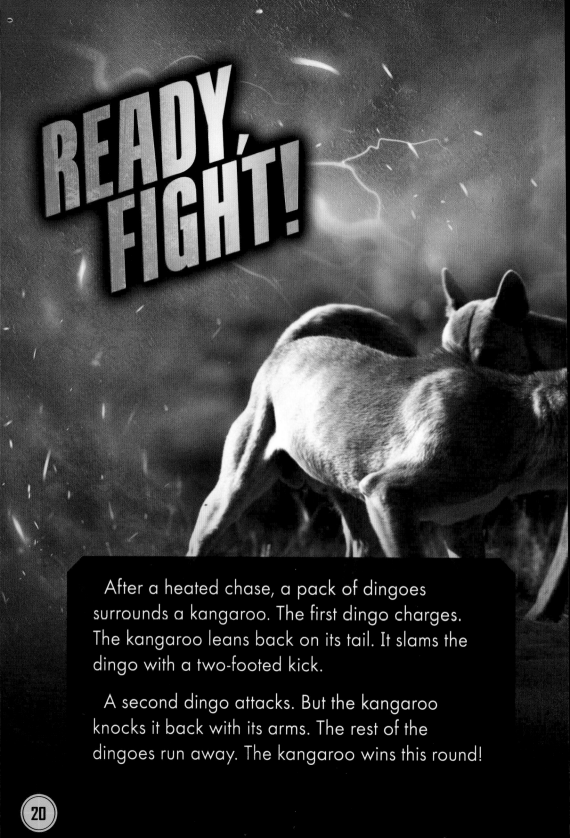

READY, FIGHT!

After a heated chase, a pack of dingoes surrounds a kangaroo. The first dingo charges. The kangaroo leans back on its tail. It slams the dingo with a two-footed kick.

A second dingo attacks. But the kangaroo knocks it back with its arms. The rest of the dingoes run away. The kangaroo wins this round!

GLOSSARY

canine teeth—long, pointed teeth that are often the sharpest in the mouth

force—the strength of an action

habitats—the homes or areas where animals prefer to live

marsupials—mammals that carry their young in a pouch on their bodies

plains—large areas of flat land

predators—animals that hunt other animals for food

prey—animals that are hunted by other animals for food

species—kinds of animals

territorial—ready to defend a home area

TO LEARN MORE

AT THE LIBRARY

Herrington, Lisa M. *Kangaroos: Amazing Jumpers*. New York, N.Y.: Children's Press, 2020.

McKinnon, Elaine. *Dingoes*. New York, N.Y.: PowerKids Press, 2017.

Murray, Julie. *Kangaroos*. Minneapolis, Minn.: Abdo Kids, 2017.

ON THE WEB

FACTSURFER

Factsurfer.com gives you a safe, fun way to find more information.

1. Go to www.factsurfer.com

2. Enter "dingo vs. kangaroo" into the search box and click Q.

3. Select your book cover to see a list of related content.

INDEX